First World War
and Army of Occupation
War Diary
France, Belgium and Germany

52 DIVISION
Divisional Troops
984 Divisional Employment Company
1 May 1919 - 31 May 1919

WO95/2895/3

The Naval & Military Press Ltd
www.nmarchive.com
Published in association with The National Archives

Published by

The Naval & Military Press Ltd

Unit 10 Ridgewood Industrial Park,

Uckfield, East Sussex,

TN22 5QE England

Tel: +44 (0) 1825 749494

www.naval-military-press.com

www.nmarchive.com

This diary has been reprinted in facsimile from the original. Any imperfections are inevitably reproduced and the quality may fall short of modern type and cartographic standards.

© Crown Copyright
Images reproduced by permission of The National Archives, London, England, 2015.

Contents

Document type	Place/Title	Date From	Date To
Heading	WO95/2895-3		
Heading	52 Div 984 Divisional Employment Coy Labour Corps 1918 May 19 only		
War Diary		01/05/1919	06/05/1919
War Diary	France	07/05/1919	31/05/1919

WO95/28485(3)

WO95/28485(3)

52 DIV

984 DIVISIONAL EMPLOYMENT Coy LABOUR CORPS.

1918 MAY to 19 ONLY

9th Divisional Employment Coy.

Army Form C. 2118.

WAR DIARY
or
INTELLIGENCE SUMMARY.
(Erase heading not required.)

May 1918

Place	Date	Hour	Summary of Events and Information	Remarks and references to Appendices
	1st		At Sea	
	2nd		do.	
	3rd		do.	
	4th		do.	
	5th		do.	
	6th		do.	
France	7th		Arrived Marseilles 0800.	
	8/9		Fournier Camp. Dozen ranks admitted to Hospital	
	10"		Entrained Marseilles 1200 for Rouen	
	11"		In Train	
	12"		Arrived Rouen 12.30. Marched to No. 10 Rest Camp.	
	13"		Entrained Rouen 1100. 1 other rank admitted to Hospital	
	14"		Arrived Étaples 0500. Marched to Rest Camp	
	15"		Entrained Étaples 0100. Arrived Romeo Camp 1500. Marched to Rest Camp	
	16"		Entrained Romeo Camp 10.30. Arrived Abbeville 2100. do.	
	17"		Entrained Abbeville 1930. 2 other ranks admitted to Hospital	
	18"		Arrived St Roi 0500. Marched to Villers Au Bois 0930. Reported to Divisional Headquarters	
	19/20		Villers Au Bois. 3 other ranks admitted to Hospital.	
	21st		114 Other Ranks Company distributed to Posts in Divisional Area.	
	22/31		Villers Au Bois. 7 other ranks admitted to Hospital	

Strength of Company. 2 Officers. 261 Other Ranks.

S. Fyffe. Lieut.
O/C 9th Divisional Employment Coy.

www.ingramcontent.com/pod-product-compliance
Lightning Source LLC
Chambersburg PA
CBHW081513160426
43193CB00014B/2677